LISTENING

IN MANY

PUBLICS

LISTENING IN MANY PUBLICS

JAY RITCHIE

Halifax | Fredericton | Picton

Library and Archives Canada Cataloguing in Publication
Title: Listening in many publics / Jay Ritchie.
Names: Ritchie, Jay Winston, 1990- author.
Identifiers: Canadiana (print) 2023059008X | Canadiana (ebook) 20230590098 | ISBN 9781778430442
  (softcover) | ISBN 9781778430459 (EPUB)
Subjects: LCGFT: Poetry.
Classification: LCC PS8635.I777 L57 2024 | DDC C811/.6—dc23

Edited by Peter Gizzi
Cover design by Megan Fildes
Interior design by Megan Fildes | Typeset in Laurentian
With thanks to type designer Rod McDonald

Invisible Publishing is committed to protecting our natural environment. As part of our efforts, both the cover and interior of this book are printed on acid-free 100% post-consumer recycled fibres.

Printed and bound in Canada.

Invisible Publishing | Halifax, Fredericton, & Picton
www.invisiblepublishing.com

Published with the generous assistance of the Canada Council for the Arts, the Ontario Arts Council, and the Government of Canada.

For Amelia, Felix, and Vera

SONNETS FROM DECIVILIZATION

One shipment: a single tusk
One shipment: two tusks
One shipment: three tusks
One shipment: four tusks
One shipment: two tusks

— ARTHUR RIMBAUD'S LAST LETTER,
written to an importer on November 9,
1891, the day before he died

1.

I came outside to see the light
On wet ground, changed
How do I explain to you that I will die?
Cinnamon on the air, I'm inside
Your room which is a rose, no one's here
I fall apart on your sofa in the early afternoon
Spring & death, spring & death
The combined effect of stress & precarious employment
The pitched-down colour of the sky
A cardboard box peeling in the rain
I reach dramatically for your hand in Target
An unspecific & crowded citizen
You speak to me like a seventh chord
I turn & stare into the resonance

2.

I turn & stare into the resonance
Of a glacial stone deposited human ages
Ago at the edge of a desiccated meadow
& in a flash you decide to trust no one—
You're like a lonesome cowboy at the start of the movie
I can hardly remember sitting in half-dark
& projecting a more exciting life for myself than this
Alone in a sea of futures, as if I won't
Be the same cowboy tomorrow
It has become a challenge lately, to get up
& slip into the stream without accelerating
To flood water overtaking cars, the present far
Outpaced by its timeless, personal consequence
Often the distance between us grows as wide as it really is

3.

The distance between us grows as wide as it really is
When I lie in bed & talk with my friend
We have our theories & do our best to articulate them
Though it's hard, to say what we mean
We discuss an immanence but our condition
Keeps changing, I sense my inability
To be totally 100% accurate in his own hesitation
Or drifting
To a seemingly unrelated topic, dinner tomorrow
Though of course this is central
To the question of living, well or otherwise, my friend
Is planning an American tour, that's all
He's ever wanted to do, tour America & make no money
I'm awake in some kind of twilight of knowing one thing for sure

4.

In some kind of twilight of knowing one thing for sure
I walk into Circle K with my one life
Running, recall the latest research shows
Atmospheric carbon reduces cognitive ability
When the Koala Bear Kare station
In the stall takes us back to desire for McDonald's
& what, in *The Cultural Logic of Late Capitalism*,
Did Jameson say
About "consumers' appetite for a world
Transformed into sheer images of itself"?
On somewhere's future condition I sink
To my knees the most certain, with absolute certainty
& nothing I order online ever lands on my doorstep
Ready to change me like that

5.

Ready to change me, like that
Aphoristic sticker on my student's laptop
I read while explaining how my face cracked
Open when I crashed my bike after therapy
So please forgive any confusion in today's lecture
On Césaire & what he calls "decivilization"
Whereby the colonial force degrades itself through violence
Today the sun shines brightly on our catastrophe
A boy punches his friend to say hello
The variegated future melts away
Outside the early park glows for workers
& tai chi practitioners in barren Angrignon lot
They seem to heal me by healing themselves
THE ONLY WAY OUT IS THROUGH

6.

"The only way out is through
The way you came in," the Enterprise rep said
You explain to me a type of orange car paint
That is also many other colours
Consider this my final poem
For some great meaning only stalls
Long enough to be looked at
When an imagined barrier   Is maintained
Have you heard
The parable of the mystic
Who preferred the sound of the orchestra tuning
Over Beethoven's Fifth Symphony?
I guess he had to sit through the whole
Thing

7.

I guess she had to sit through the whole thing
Forever waking up into the soft fact of self
Sublate the need for actualization
Into a new way of wearing old clothes
The colour red rising
Slightly above the other colours
A military plane passes overhead
It's not the fault of the weather
You explain to the dead sparrow
That poetry is   A concave space in the words
& the lovelier paramour of our method
Photographs the same
While occupying the very frame
As if they were on a loop

8.

As if they were on a loop
The days sync in & out of phase
Our iambic advance through thresholds
Of gain, these lines are crucibles of joy
Forged in the abjection of human will
A language upon which the future is hinged
Somehow you make it to March, again
Why can't I find a place to live for a couple years?
It's so embarrassing to be alive
I wake up in a strange place but recognize the trees
Like seeing a word spelled correctly in a mirror
Funny, I have that feeling again
Of a funnel above my head
The world pouring in

9.

The world pours in
I don't want to live   I want to live
In a state of constant ecstasy
Yes, yes I do
I am afraid of being hurt
& I love to know intimate details
About different cities
I have my whole life in my head
Can't you see it?
I remember learning to read & being confused
By sections in the newspaper
Sports Entertainment Politics Arts
Aren't they all the same thing?
Music

10.

Music activates my banal surroundings, that
Wide glissando of being, finally, nothing
A little progress made in these passing offices
Threading an invisible needle with the mute
Braid of an intention, yes
I meant to call you before it frayed & say
You're invited to my party
It's a celebration of my undying love for you
You don't have to care   You just have to show up
I think of men dying alone in their refusal
Rivers easily ruin their borders
I close an ad for ad-blocking software
& abandon my fascination with dialectics
Rabbit hole at the end of a rabbit hole

11.

Rabbit hole at the end of a rabbit hole
Here I am at the bottom of poetry
Looking out over persona's sundered edge
& um would it bother you
If I laid down & just gave up, whatever it is
I am doing, gave up completely?
You learn to change
Then you learn to change how you change
Today the future is where I breathe in
The need for a common language to talk to you
Beyond anything I can articulate
Moody at the dinner table, but sometimes
When we rent a car & drive through the woods
I experience tranquility

12.

I experience tranquility
Then the experience moves outside me
Some actors are favourites of directors
Their performances are less about character
Than the possibility they present
To us, to be various
In our lives, a chance at renewal
Today I am depressed
Though the sun is brightest it has been
All year, & it's warm, breezy
I fear I have made a terrible mistake
The white picket fence of my neighbour   Is not a symbol
For idyllic, middle-class life with liberal values
It is to keep me off his lawn

13.

To keep me off his lawn
The landlord stood staring, white with rage
Outside the spring snow   Revels in me
I hear it falling on the grass
It sounds like fire
I am alone in my room
Writing another essay
Composed of small, atmospheric changes in mood
Even gradual change has a sudden shift
When the new rhythm eclipses the old
The possibilities jump out of their metre
If you knew you had a hand in your own destruction
If you could hold each snowflake in a storm
If the storm itself were shelter

14.

If the storm itself were shelter
We wouldn't have to get away from the storm
For a bit, get away in a book or TV show
After all, we know they, too, are a part
Parts of it, & you are part of all of this & more
Including war, including war
But this isn't about that, about how it's all nested
& escape is impossible, there is no outside experience
This is about how you are taking ceramics classes
This spring, how you are sitting there at the wheel
You've always wanted to sit at, sculpting
Sculpting into the night, so devoted that when leaving
The studio exhausted you were surprised
To come outside & see the light

LISTENING IN MANY PUBLICS

...it is to this zone of occult instability where the people dwell that we must come; and it is there that our souls are crystallized and that our perceptions and our lives are transfused with light.

—FRANTZ FANON, *THE WRETCHED OF THE EARTH*

1.

    grooves in the cold, wet grass
made by a swinging gate

I thought about early textiles,
the materialization of social order

Fake flowers   Real feelings

2.

Become   It's work
When the motion
means to leave with oneness

"Your most opposite person your greatest teacher."

I also heard
night wind knocked out the power in regions
not far from here, though far-sounding,
regions that voted differently

3.

The trees are not metaphorical.
They are not what you lack
or the lack you desire

       a heron alights on a small mound of earth
protruding from the confluence of rivers,
initiating a subtle change in behaviour

To break the pattern first you must accept it:
Say, "Hello pattern."

Today I saw the Coca-Cola truck again

Discover nothing & remember

4.

There are also changes
There is hope these changes
I approach the corner building ready to ascend

What is positioned directly opposite you now?

& what is just to your side, prepared to alter
the angle of approach?

There is resolve   window sashes   the stone
that keeps the weight of the building from collapsing
onto the windows

A weight that lifts itself.

5.

The line is the surface
& it is the bottom   Below that opens onto heaven

     of culture nested inside tragedy,
comprehensible or rationalized only through
grief for what was lost & is longed for
via the signifiers of loss & what you would
be if not for

Experience mediated by how to convey it

6.

The non-accumulation of every novelty

7.

A field of dandelions
& the transmission towers above
& the building demolished
& the building that goes on

The archive reveals little
of what is sought & changes
the framing of the question

Words on their own are history

The city, so-called,
exerts by itself

8.

Metals in the scrapyard
Use & with no function
The people

People speak to what is needed
what is specific   & whole

Casting attention to the past
Time comes around
to exist when it is seen

9.

The limitations
of history as sediment

The view through the apartment blocks
& later beyond them
Having arrived there
in this old place
The many varied expressions of ruin
The long twentieth century

The loss of a sense of what it looks like
& finally   Appearing

To keep one problem
is called economics

10.

Received   Ideals of beauty
                                I fault
early builders who found philosophies
to flatter their engines

        brutal categorization
Another element made invisible
& more easily enforced

Consensus reality flowing inward

The phenomenology of objects
altered by metrics

Careful   from behind barriers
From outside a prolonged scream

11.

The colour of the bricks
The timing of the traffic lights
They all contribute to the narrative

The narrative of being through possession

I feel already my childhood yards
     worlds, the empty lot with tall reeds
taller than any of us pretending
it was a desert, the sand-yellow
of the reeds.

       It was because it was not

12.

The reeds
The kids going to school
The transitive relation
between boundaries & grammar

The grammar of boundaries
The intersubjective
The conditional

13.

    coupling & decoupling
from the great distance of affect
that is not defined by nation but remains limited by it

All boundaries sunken inward

Here I go feeling wider

When I spoke of my childhood
the graininess of the room increased

14.

Hand-me-down curricula
construct the landscape

      at the border I faced the guard. The border guard
At the border
I lied through my particulars. The details
      detail in the inquiry up close
Just texture   depth   Presence
You are also this   Close to the method

Farm implements
rusting in the earth

15.

In a dream
they were taking the Empire State Building apart
beam by beam, moving it back from the eroding cliff-face
like a lighthouse. A voice called out for the taxi to stop

It was cool, it started
to rain. The exposition bled
into the plot. A state of uncommon unrest

    & how,
going forward, the silence will break

16.

a way of going forward that is not progressive

At every juncture   A new order of magnitude

Factory smoke across the water
blowing east   Seed-carrying wind
Need   the engine of survival
& of loss

17.

      your shaking hand
on the shuddering wheel

& the many paths you walked
& the many people you met

Cannons behind the seawall
Surveillance towers   The unmet

      distant mechanized echo

Dragging your luggage
into the room, giving up
everything inside

18.

Your position in relation
to the meaning-making
each day presents

Visible from a plane of action

     blossoming vulnerable   out there

Listening in many publics

Not truth   but the truth you've been told
swallowed by the hard power of telling
what it is, how it looks, how it feels

19.

Monetized individuals   Apologists
with an ethic of immutability
talk on the panel

"generates wealth with a combination of debt instruments,"

    soft mechanized hum

Nothingness capitulates to somethingness

20.

Need is very bright in the square of human error *

You sense its contours   The locales
that seemed so far off once again woven
into the fabric of your circumstance

Wild deer eating acorns

        how it felt to lose
what you never wanted

In some moments the child part comes up

Consciousness the speed of becoming
aware of perception

21.

It is practical, it is the practice
of theoretical concerns & the return
to a future self

    the joining of never & always occurs constantly,
it is a has-happened, an is

22.

A collective reciprocity:

I live on a street near a park.
The street has a name,
& the park has a name.
The oil stain & the pines
are not represented, though
their physicality remains
altered by these names

"9th"

"Prospect"

23.

The Law of the Negation of the Negation

     need is very bright in the human

So do. So one commits
to being undone. So the air
hangs between buildings
convincing the people of something
     it is something
The something of people in the path
of the wind   People
who, over breakfast downtown before work,
say, "something is changing"
     "I forgot something"
Something is clearing
& you do

24.

A mightier push from forces above the line of beauty
turned loss into a place. From the edges
I forged a cable of lift

Natural rhythms   chatter, squawk   water
It is because of difference that depth emerges

25.

    emergent strategy without a common referent
against the void of property
& the social relations that follow

Cast aside an anxious-avoidant attachment to the state

The vines grow   Think
a separate transmission

Tenants gathered on the dirt to plant vegetables
& share resources

26.

Sunbeams on rhizomes
The blinking open spaces

Entire branches across the street
Want for the state of unwanting

The song of the red-winged blackbird
almost digital

Cutting through the grass
I felt a quieter energy move in

27.

I waver
dissonant & clear
moored in wandering harbours
having done some grief-work

    & to speak on them
is to speak on our image

Remnants of rain on concrete
Air makes the crane appear bent

28.

It looks like how we live
when we live with our calamity

     some levity in doing away with terms
Surrender   Persevere   both-and

The incidentals in what is sought after
defined by the material conditions

Sequences that rise from overlap of sequence

I write the exact phrase to hear
what cannot be said

29.

     particulars corralled into generalities:
The messages over the airwaves are for you
when you are become someone else

Sameness happening is difference

The deepening influence of enjoyment
     kitchen mornings, the instrument resting on the bed

30.

    along the plaza beneath awnings
past butchers & salons
looking for what would distinguish my subjection

I made my way to the speaker
who can give a name to each phenomenon:

    the cost of entry   the sky without a stain
emblems on granite   the Latin names of birds
All converging on the same point of reference

A turgid concentration of language
in service of policy   To deny
& make foundational

The reality it describes so common as to go unnoticed

31.

A relation of denial
when nourishment is under guard

      & many people
many of them go on   Past ache's horizon

& it in itself composed of variations
& not singular

32.

With no referent for how to function
outside of anxiety, how unlikely to glimpse
an image of the life after

A following behind that does not replicate
No apprehension travelling beyond signposts

In a dream of surveillance, who is watching?

Not to worry   To take action instead

33.

Blue crescendos   blonde concrete
The bottom
        gleaned between the structures

Impatient to arrive

        satellites banks   hospitals
sewers, billboards, highways, aqueducts

Unintelligible distance   Your position

34.

A newness of relative difference
inside the developed façade

To speak on it is a surfactant

The glass breaks
The frame expands

    the entire force drifts slightly. Its
momentum perceptible only after stoppage
in the anti-teleology of elemental shifts

35.

The old way thereby
reproducing the closure

The past rises up   Erratic

The self & the habit split. A morning
      fully extrinsic

36.

Reminder: You
did not lose what
you never were

& so cannot find
what is not there

You must make it
You must
Make it

37.

The pressure clears
& starting out into the cooler morning air
I thought about decay

Peeling tiles   Rebirth

The messages came through as pulsations
which turned my attention around various corners
but was never more
than the strangeness of life itself—

38.

& I walked very closely to it
jutting out with the possibility
     quiet, terrible quiet
& I saw it at times hovering
as if it had escaped me & was not
sovereign. At times the exigence
eclipses the form   The form
at times takes the shape
of things

Things I have
mistaken

39.

Not taken
Not used
Not desiring
Not this once

A lit window   Adjustments
made to iconography
to signal the start of dream-training
    & still it is not safe

40.

       the trees & streets
are a little different

I have a view on a life.

Trace the contour of a rising doubt
Bury sunlight in the patch

I also glance outward, knowing
it is the second time
the first time around

Your agon to embrace
This untidy sensation

THE IMAGE WORLD

...we got to / come out from behind the image

—DIANE DI PRIMA, "REVOLUTIONARY LETTER #11"

PART I

1.

We are now in a place that is unlike you.

The wide urgency
beside an open August window,
where outside the leaves are blue, just
after the sun's eye has shut,
heat pulsing up from your street,
& you will be uncomplicated
from this moment forward.

Look:
The wooden house in the complex
gets darker when it rains.

You see it
as a consequence of the moon,
another way to feel earthbound—
like north, south, east, & west,
a bandage pressed evenly
across the wound.

Recover.

Dress.

Ride on the back of a black horse
to Albany.

The black horse is a legacy
of carbon emissions & interest-bearing loans.
Albany is Albany.

2.

Outside the city limit,
the cream is thick.
The boars are rutting.

You meet a multidisciplinary artist.

You spot wild onions at the edge of the forest.

Swiftly overhead move the clouds.

3.

Lonely at the front door to anywhere,
the city seems to travel with you.

The rails wet with predicated rain.

"You are a generous individual
in a system that rewards selfishness."

The multidisciplinary artist leaves a voicemail
you listen to in the dark.

Centuries gather in the dawning
middle distance to debate our worship.
Is it history.

4.

The sentries distribute a pamphlet
on the ontological paradox
of arrival.

"Arrival always coincides with the dissolution of your
destination."

Screens in the concourse advertise imminent departures
& local growers.

You are pushed through a ceremony of questions
into a grammar of settled tenses
congruent only to language
in settled spaces.

How close the period is to the end of our sentence.

The trees beside the street
an ellipsis, a way to say *hold on,*
a march of unbroken thoughts
that lead to the next page of forest
in protest.

Today is bustling & already begun.

Before you, the square
with tents pitched close as trees.

Unguarded, the image turns
at the speed of possibility.

Drums fill busy agendas with worry.

Dreams grow teeth filed by dreamers
on the whetstone of morning.

You take a video camera out of your bag
& start filming: the encampment, the sky.
Nothing looks like how it feels,
pink & articulated.

Absent from the visual the low rumble of trucks,
the lower rumble of a shift.

A philosopher addresses the crowd.

Reporters note facts on their devices.

A dancer points to a sign
whose message can only be read
through movement.

5.

Your calendar dissolves.

It's overcast.

You rest your head against a brick wall.

It's overcast.

A corrugated firmament hangs over the exchanges:
wages, sustenance, wages, sustenance.

Overcast.

You feel a great deal, a great variety,
on your walk to & from the supermarket.

"There's time to cavil, standing still," the dancer said.

It was overcast.

It's midnight, & the supermarket looks like an airport.

6.

In the country,
fences appear to repeat as you pass,
their boundary doubling,
dividing in from out, have from haven't,
is from was, a cut in space
that generates time.

Here the grace of a chance to come even closer.

You've been invited to a house in this rural town,
though you cannot find the address
while walking through a strange neighbourhood
in the dark (it is winter)
& you suspect you have been fooled:
there is no house, you have no friends,
this is but another attempt at distance.

Fixity is a fiction
when you live somewhere one year at a time,
two, you must lie to all the clerks
& believe a permanent address
is out there waiting for you.

In this impermanence live all the decisions you made
that were not rational & could not be explained,
decisions that if you could explain them
you wouldn't have chased them,
quests deemed unacceptable;
you were after you in a reckless way
that laughed in the face of all philosophy,
distant language
& its permanent address.

7.

The image surges in a clearing.

You are no passive agent.

The sun bounces off your jewellery.

The generators of City B
hum beside the floodgates.

Rusted pipes leak
onto rusted fittings piled in corners.
Abandoned cars stretch for miles.

Your childhood trespasses churn
with the sticks & plastic
before the release of the river.

Photographs capture the power station
in sustainable development drag.

Fallen leaves reveal places
where the grid goes unconnected.

8.

In an exurb of City B,
the oil refinery burns its surplus.

It looks like a birthday cake.

9.

Within the park groups are forming.

You sit with a translator
on a bench across from a fountain.

There is so much you want to say.

Intervals between the water speak
of how your sacrifices have made
a possible future instantly fade.

"Naming what is there without obscuring what is not
is the fundamental challenge of translation,"
the translator says.

The fountain honours French murderers
from the seventeenth century.
Its inflected stone acquires a politic
vacated only by destruction.

"Reappropriation," the translator suggests.

Down in the quarry, the ceremony
has already started.

10.

Water makes its home in the rock
one sound at a time.

Industry retreats to the interior.

There.

The scaffolding used for extraction stands, still,
a remainder.

Your work is the image of work, a working image.

The photographer
quotes Barthes to the flower arrangements.
"This-will-be" & "this-has-been."

White wine in the afternoon.

The air textured like fabric, a warp
in the pattern of lack.

11.

In the estuary, birds rest on reeds
that bend like question marks.

The image speaks.

Letters & words seem to slip
out of their function,
placeholders for better, truer symbols,
symbols with meanings
that are beyond awareness.

In a red patch of mud
you meet a scholar.

The scholar expresses regret
over the change in direction
of a major automobile manufacturer.

The tide goes out.

Leaves flash from blue to red in the quickening wind.

The world waits to be undiscovered.

12.

At the end of the dock,
the late lights of City B
obscured by fog.

An intermittent beeping floats across the water.

A barge of dying smoke alarms
drifts toward the transfer station.

Disoriented, the kingfishers launch themselves
against the glass panes
of the new conservatory.

Underwater, the trout breathe laced air.

Here you stand on someone else's horizon,
one point in a projection
of what is to come.

13.

Sounds from land
carry across the water.

You are welcomed
by the cradling embrace of waves.
Stars reflect on the waves' surface,
breathing like a blanket
of tiny lungs.

Sea & sky merge,
the horizon turns vertical
then disappears inside you.

At every moment of engagement
the rules of engagement change.

14.

The image of a swan slides out of the reeds.

You know in French a swan
is *cygne*, homophonous with *signe*, a sign;
the sign's beak points inland.

Sharp, then soft, the grass thins, hisses.

Events once isolated from one another in time
reveal themselves as connected,
your loss in fact a sedulous agent
that has risen in the distance
in the form of an abandoned textile mill.

Inside, a temple to the image.

15.

History, divided into floors.

What is most distant in time
feels nearest in spirit.

To relay these ancient visions,
a hectoring language is sometimes applied.
The curator hands you a pamphlet.

"An artist is one who turns error into unrepeatable origination."

Images exhale proposals from their frames.

You think this
is what perfect thinking looks like:
each shape no shape but itself,
every brushstroke going only its own way forever,
the composite a streak of colour
speeding through timeless time.

To leave a mark behind a brush must bend
when it meets the canvas.

16.

At night the mountains are still visible,
darker than the surrounding darkening sky,
emerging as they sink.

No cars.

All the stores closed.

A reproduction from the museum
sits behind the glass façade of a gallery.

A house with all its lights on near the top of the hill.

17.

You come with three or four perfect thoughts
to the summit.

Virga can be seen many miles away,
weather you interpret
as the oncoming texture of your affect.

You locate yourself at once
as a node of great influence
acting along many intersecting lines & planes.

The door to the house is already open.

The guests nod or ignore you
as you move through the house whose dimensions
you recall the moment they are revealed:
two beds in the basement,
an attic with a door
that leads to an attic with a door.

In the sitting room the guests have gathered
to watch an Agnès Varda film, but can't decide which.
When they discuss *Cléo from 5 to 7*
you keep thinking it's called
Cléo from 9 to 5, so you say nothing.

There is a book on the table called *The Book*.
It has an image of itself on the cover,
creating an infinitely repeating pattern.

Every house you've ever lived in
is part of this house,
but you are a guest.

It's a kind of negative freedom:
the traces you left behind are gone,
& nothing is suddenly in your hands
in place of a boundary.

A chance for you to start over.

You read *The Book*
& glance at the bulbs of frozen ice
on the wires outside, mistaking them for lights.

Black birds dive down to the street.

You have failed.

Out there in the thin layer
between the world & the image,
a place that is in here,
a thin layer between yesterday & the errands
of the coming morning,
you have failed.

The easy grace of air
passing over a candle.

18.

Trash collects into a shape
in the pattern of your imperfect thinking.

At dawn
there is what you see,
& there is what you remember
after the sight is gone.

Images linger, distort the new seeing.

You grieve for all the gravestones
locked to their name-ridden bodies
in the nameless light of day.

The drugstore is open.

A small maple lined with snow
beside a white propane tank
in the employee break area.

You pass through rows of promises:
"Nighttime relief."
"Advanced healing."
"Pure body."
"Total relief."

Your body stays unmet, a place
to put personhood while locating
that distant bell-like sound.

The burning earth slicked
with transactional exchanges.

19.

Thrust headlong into a remedy.

A nail of light strikes the roof of the hospital.

The nurse can get you medications,
if you want them.

The therapist said, "Adjustment Disorder,"
for billing purposes.
You ask for clarification
& are set up with a hearing test.

A recorded voice,
in American English, says:
"Hot dog."
"Ice cream."
"Toothbrush."
"Football."
"Drugstore."
"Cowboy."
"Airplane."

You refuse to cast its clinical spell
& are brought to a higher room.

Another word reaches you
from across that reoccurring distance.

Cold radiating from the windowpane.

From your position above the earth
you watch the water hurry seaward
under transmission towers.

You could not find a harder edge to rest your life on.

20.

Your convalescing spectacle
slips out the back door.

A warm air is blowing down the mountains.

The air so thick you are eating it,
getting full on breathing air.

The water full of signals.

The perfect future reassembles in your seeing before you see it
& you come to voice with the grammar
of resisting centuries to come.

PART II

You will place a chair in the garden for anyone to use.

You will remember the world & everyone in it.

The jar will come unstuck, the jar with sand around the rim.

You will leave the clay pots out in the rain.

No calculation will omit the very soil.

No difference will be negligible.

The breeze will pass as if through you.

You will never hold the toy, unless the game is one of holding.

You will be more playful for all the work that remains to be done.

You will be more free for knowing what has bounded your imagination.

Coming back to that same field you will see how the angle has changed.

The vector both curved & straight.

You will move apartments again & see your possessions in boxes.

You will recall a former professor, lecturing on Deleuze & Guattari, using her table as an example of "the rhizomatic."

You will come to sit at your own table in the morning & forget you have already taken it apart.

You will see at last "the image of thought," looking at the packing tape & spackling on the floor.

See the grain in the wood as seasons of push.

Every tree more than its taxon.

Music that comes from the bedroom will sound like it's coming from outside.

You will recall the world as it was on the day your loved one left it.

You will mourn their days unseen, & your days to come.

You will mourn the days past, & remember mourning is also a celebration.

The bloom will not break down.

You will survive a transition period of a year that fades into another transition period.

The question of living never once surrendered.

You will find yourself sitting at a rough wooden table in a small country shack, opening the envelope.

There is a painting on the wall of a chicken, a chicken unlike any you've seen.

The chicken is in profile, has a Mona Lisa smile & bluish feathers.

No artist signature is visible.

The ideas of things will not hinder your view of them.

In this pellucid state of non-attribution you will greet all sights, not just naïf chicken art.

The asphalt in the road will speak a language you used to know.

& anyway language has always been an exercise in reading negative space.

You will get to a point where all other points feel equally distant, & this will be a comfort.

Not for lack of wanting, you will receive enduring pleasure in a bare room.

You will go to your project after great sacrifice only to find your project already complete.

You will be capable of enacting possibilities you couldn't
have dreamed

& awake again in the same life you might think of trains &
falling asleep at a window,

waking up to a world outside, different from the one you left
behind.

NOTES

The epigraph from Rimbaud can be found in *Arthur Rimbaud: Complete Works*, translated by Paul Schmidt.

"Decivilization" is an extension of Aimé Césaire's neologism "decivilize," coined in his 1950 essay *Discourse on Colonialism*, translated by Joan Pinkham.

The Fredric Jameson quote is from *Postmodernism, or, The Cultural Logic of Late Capitalism*.

The phrase "to be various in our lives" is a riff on the line "Grace / to be born and live as variously as possible" from Frank O'Hara's poem "In Memory of My Feelings." The line is also his epitaph.

The quote from Frantz Fanon can be found in *The Wretched of the Earth*, translated by Constance Farrington.

The phrase "emergent strategy" is from the book *Emergent Strategy: Shaping Change, Changing Worlds* by adrienne maree brown.

The phrase "quests deemed unacceptable" is taken from Aimé Césaire's essay "Isidore Ducasse, Comte de Lautréamont," published in *Tropiques* no. 6–7, 1943, translated by Annette Smith and Clayton Eshleman.

"This-will-be" and "this-has-been" is from Roland Barthes's *Camera Lucida: Reflections on Photography*, translated by Richard Howard.

The relationship between *signe* and *cygne* is lifted from the section "Urania | Astronomy" of Theresa Hak Kyung Cha's *Dictee*.

ACKNOWLEDGEMENTS

I am grateful to the following people, whose generosity brought this book into existence: my editor, Peter Gizzi, who nurtured this work from the very beginning; Ocean Vuong, who championed its hybrid forms as an unforgettable thesis advisor; Dara Barrois/Dixon, who provided advice and direction along the way. To Norm Nehmetallah, Megan Fildes, Jules Wilson, and the rest of the Invisible team, for making this book possible. To the long poem group: Jack Chelgren, Ell Davis, Amanda Dahill-Moore, and Jamie Thomson, for getting together in attics and living rooms and going on for longer than we should. To my friends, family, collaborators, too many to mention: without you, no poetry. Most of all to Henrika, for talking every morning, and for laughing every night.

Thank you to the editors of *EVENT*, *The Dalhousie Review*, *Vallum*, *Caret*, and *Violet Indigo Blue, etc.*, where many of these poems were first published.

JAY RITCHIE is a writer, editor, teacher, and McGill English PhD student. Author of the poetry collection *Cheer Up, Jay Ritchie* (Coach House Books), a collection of short stories, and a poetry chapbook, he has an MFA in Poetry from UMass Amherst and was the Assistant Editor for Metatron Press and Managing Editor of *Vallum Magazine.* Jay lives in Tio'tia:ke / Montreal.

INVISIBLE PUBLISHING produces fine Canadian literature for those who enjoy such things. As an independent, not-for-profit publisher, we work to build communities that sustain and encourage engaging, literary, and current writing.

Invisible Publishing has been in operation for over a decade. We released our first fiction titles in the spring of 2007, and our catalogue has come to include works of graphic fiction and nonfiction, pop culture biographies, experimental poetry, and prose.

We are committed to publishing writers with diverse perspectives. In acknowledging historical and systemic barriers, and the limits of our existing catalogue, we emphatically encourage writers from LGBTQ2SIA+ communities, Indigenous writers, and writers of colour to submit their work.

Invisible Publishing is also home to the Bibliophonic series of music books and the Throwback series of CanLit reissues.

If you'd like to know more, please get
in touch: info@invisiblepublishing.com